SUPER DC HEROES

BATMAN

HARLEY QUINN'S SHOCKING SURPRISE

WRITTEN BY
BLAKE A. HOENA

ILLUSTRATED BY
DAN SCHOENING

BATMAN CREATED BY
BOB KANE

Raintree

www.raintreepublishers.co.uk
Visit our website to find out
more information about
Raintree books.

Phone 0845 6044371
Fax +44 (0) 1865 312263
Email myorders@capstonepub.co.uk

Customers from outside the UK please telephone +44 1865 312262

Raintree is an imprint of Capstone Global Library Limited,
a company incorporated in England and Wales having its registered office at
7 Pilgrim Street, London, EC4V 6LB – Registered company number: 6695582

"Raintree" is a registered trademark of Pearson Education Limited, under licence to
Capstone Global Library Limited

First published by Stone Arch Books in 2010
First published in hardback in the United Kingdom in 2010
Paperback edition first published in the United Kingdom in 2010

Art D...or: Bob Lent...
...opies: Bri...n Bascl...
UK Editor: Vaarunika Dharmapala
Originated by Capstone Global Library Ltd
Printed and bound in China by Leo Paper Products Ltd

ISBN 978 1 406215 49 6 (hardback)
14 13 12 11 10
10 9 8 7 6 5 4 3 2 1

ISBN 978 1 406215 63 2 (paperback)
14 13 12 11 10
10 9 8 7 6 5 4 3 2 1

British Library Cataloguing in Publication Data
A full catalogue record for this book is available from the British Library.

CONTENTS

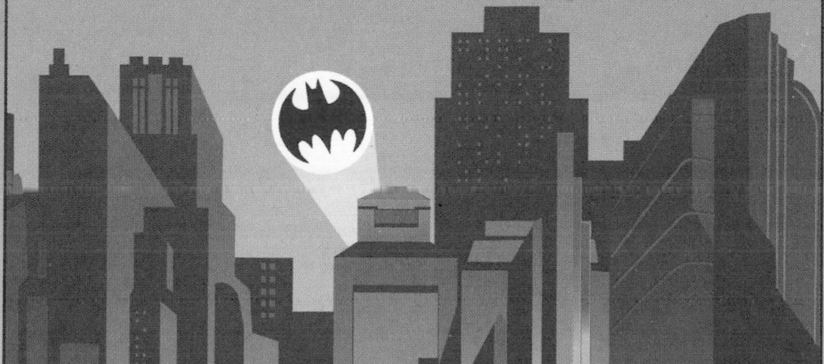

CHAPTER 1

BOY WONDER

Timothy Drake plopped down in a chair and looked up at the Batcave's main monitor. The screen displayed a map of Gotham City. Near its centre, a red light flashed, signalling a crime in progress.

Tim slumped further into the chair. He should be there helping catch the crooks. After all, he was secretly Robin – one half of the Dynamic Duo. He had been on the bus headed home from school when the alarm went off, so the Caped Crusader had left without him.

"I hate riding the bus," Tim complained.

Batman's butler, Alfred Pennyworth, entered the cave. Alfred walked up to Tim and placed a tray of sandwiches next to the unmasked Boy Wonder.

"No use grumbling, Master Timothy. I'm sure there will be other crimes for you to foil," Alfred said. "Until then, why don't you work on your homework?"

Tim grabbed a sandwich and stuffed half into his mouth. "Fine," he mumbled.

Tim sat behind a desk. He pressed his hand against a panel. **POP!** A keyboard appeared. Tim started typing as Alfred walked away.

"If I remember correctly," Alfred said, "you have an oral presentation due this Friday on coral reef habitats."

"Yeah," Tim muttered. "Clown fish, electric eels, sharks, and stuff. No biggy."

As Alfred walked out of the room, Tim pushed another panel on the desk. **CLICK!** A controller appeared from a secret compartment. He typed in a few commands, and the game *Crime Fighters* flashed on the screen.

"If I can't help Batman fight real criminals," Tim whispered, "at least I can take on some cyber crooks."

Suddenly, the screen in front of Tim went blank. "Hey!" he yelled. "What happened?"

Then, on the monitor, the map of Gotham City reappeared. A red light blinked on a warehouse in the northern part of town, signalling that an alarm had been set off.

"Could be a robbery," Tim said excitedly. "I'd better check it out."

Tim jumped out of his chair. He quickly put on his Robin gear and then ran to the Batcave's garage. His scooter was parked off to one side.

It's no Batcycle, Tim thought, *but at least it's cooler than riding the bus.*

After hopping on the scooter, Tim zoomed out of the Batcave. Within moments, he was racing across the Robert Kane Memorial Bridge and entering Gotham City limits.

Robin radioed Batman while on his way to the crime scene. "I'm headed to the warehouse district," Robin spoke into his headset. "There's a possible burglary in progress there."

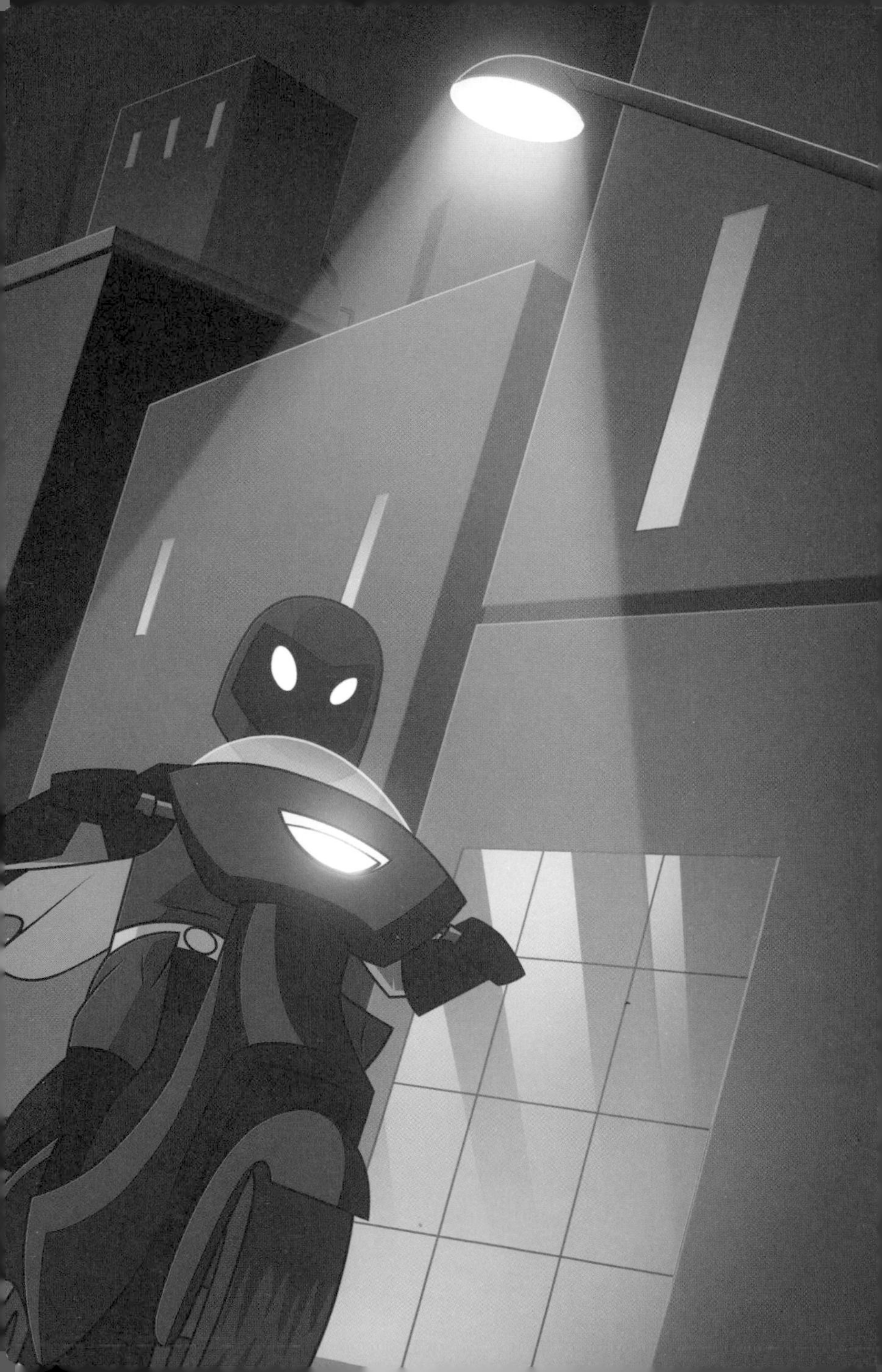

"I've almost finished here," Batman replied. "I'll meet you there."

"Sure thing," Robin said.

Minutes later, Robin rolled to a halt. He was about half a block from the warehouse. The sun was setting. Shadows were growing long. Everyone had headed home for the night, and the area was quiet, almost spooky. Robin hopped off his scooter and parked it against the side of a building.

Sticking to the shadows, he sneaked up to the warehouse. He crept up to a window and peered in. There was nothing to see inside. No crime. No lights. No people. Nothing. Just some wooden crates and rusted barrels.

Robin ducked around the back of the warehouse. The rear door was slightly open.

Robin peeked inside. He wondered if he should wait for Batman.

Well, Robin thought, *if Batman can bust some thieves on his own, I should be able to check out an empty warehouse.*

Quietly, Robin slipped through the open door. He ducked behind a barrel and listened. All was quiet except for the wind brushing up against the side of the building. He peeked around the barrel and saw only shadows surrounding him.

Disappointed, Robin stood up and walked carelessly to the centre of the warehouse. A waning ray of sunlight lit the area where he stood.

"I can't believe it," Robin said, kicking at the dust on the floor. "Batman gets to break up a heist, and I get a false alarm."

High above, a dark shadow tiptoed across a narrow platform. It stopped and grabbed the end of a rope in one hand. The other hand held a crowbar. Silently, the figure leaped off the platform.

As the shadowy figure swung down, Robin heard something whistle through the air. He turned and looked up just in time to see a crowbar flying towards him.

Robin fell to the ground with a thud. He had been knocked unconscious.

The dark figure let go of the rope, twirled through the air, and skillfully landed a few feet from Robin. It slowly walked over to the fallen hero, one hand still holding the crowbar.

Then the figure stepped into the light.

First, the leggings of a black and red costume became visible. Slowly, as it moved closer, the light crept up its body, revealing a female figure. And then, finally, a smiling face covered in white makeup with a black mask. It was Harley Quinn, one of Batman's most dangerous enemies!

HAHAHAHA! Her laugh echoed through the warehouse.

"Well, well, Boy Blunder," Harley Quinn said. "You fell right into my trap!"

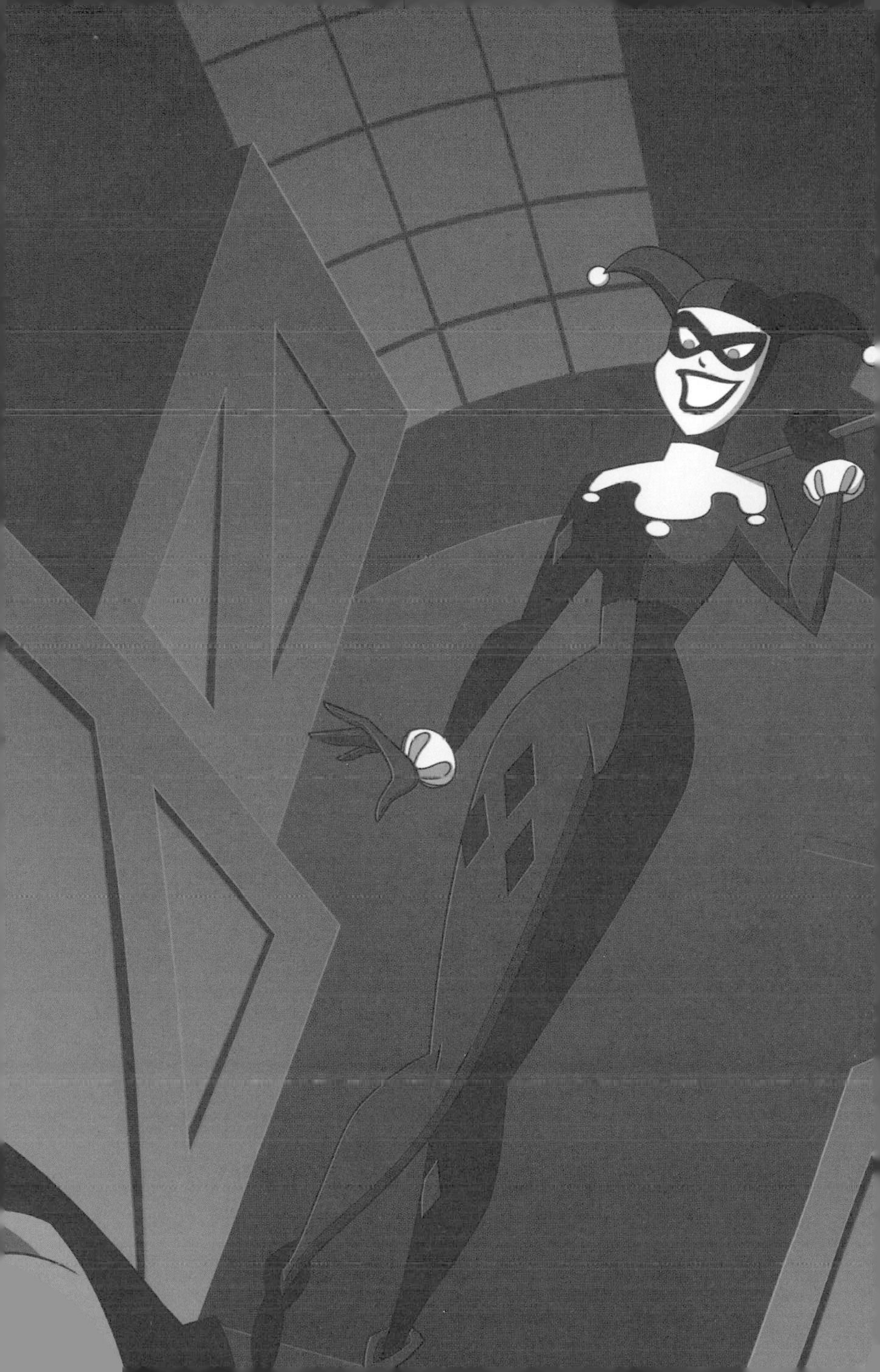

CHAPTER 2

FALSE ALARM

"Someone tampered with the warning system," Batman explained to Detective Renee Montoya.

"So this was just a false alarm?" the detective asked.

They stood in the doorway of the Pearl Emporium. Outside, parked on the street, were three police cars, their lights reflecting off the shop's windows. Around the area, several police officers wandered about. Some chatted with bystanders while others looked for clues.

"Someone went to a lot of work just to play a prank," Montoya said.

"I'm afraid this may be some sort of diversion," Batman said, scanning the rooftops of nearby stores. "Better ask Commissioner Gordon to keep a couple of police cars in the area."

"We'll be ready for whatever this practical joker has planned," Renee said.

Just then, Batman received the call from Robin telling him about the break-in.

"I need to go," Batman told Renee, as he turned towards his Batcycle.

"Do you want back up?" she asked.

Batman leaped on to the cycle. "No, Robin and I can handle this one," he said. "You see if you can find any clues about who set off the false alarm."

RUMMMMMMMBLE! The Batcycle's engine roared to life, and Batman sped off into the night.

The wind screamed in his ears as Batman raced through Gotham City. He was going so fast that he almost didn't see the black van blocking the road. His tyres squealed as he slid to a halt.

SKREEE-EEE-EEECH!

Batman stopped alongside the motionless van. He peeked through a window to see if the driver was okay. But strangely, no one was inside.

It could be stolen, Batman thought. *But it seems like the van was left here on purpose.*

On the side of the van was a big picture of a colourful fish. Under the fish were the words "Fish 'N' Stuff."

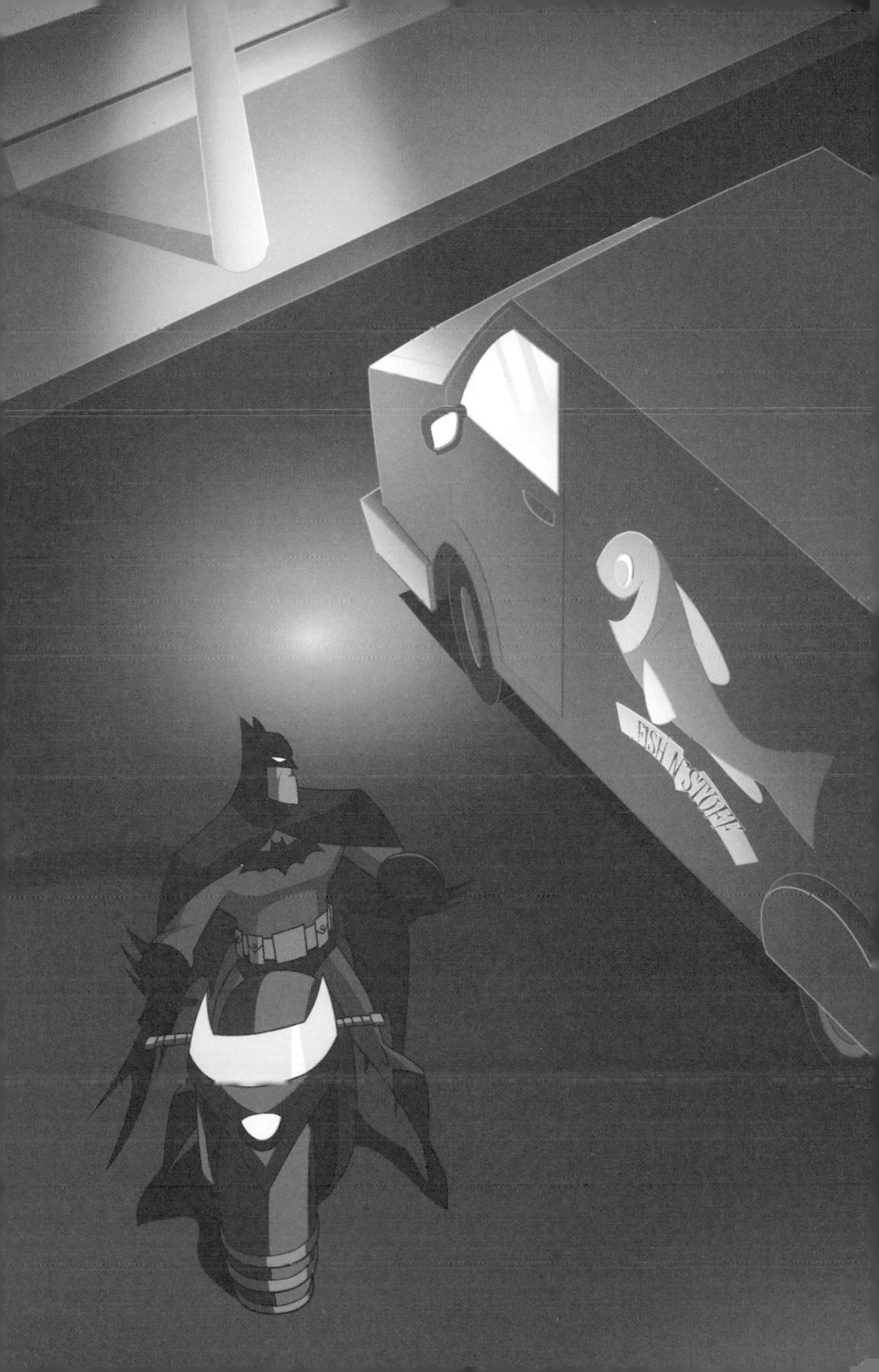
FISH N' STORE

"Alfred," Batman spoke into his headset. "There's a van blocking Emerson Avenue. It might be stolen. Could you send a tow truck?"

"I'll get right on it," Alfred replied.

Batman threw a flare down in front of the van to warn any approaching motorists. Then he sped off on the Batcycle. Within minutes, he reached the warehouse district. When Batman saw Robin's scooter, he let the Batcycle coast to a stop next to it.

"Robin, I'm here," Batman said into his headset. He heard only static in response.

"Robin?" Batman repeated.

Nothing.

Batman leaned over Robin's scooter, placing a hand near the exhaust pipe.

Still warm, Batman thought. *Robin was here recently.*

Staying in the shadows, Batman sneaked up to one of the warehouse windows. He peered in, but saw nothing inside.

Quickly, he darted around the back and found the door still slightly open. Once inside, Batman grabbed a torch from his Utility Belt. Flicking it on, he noticed everything was covered in dust, as if the warehouse had been abandoned many years ago.

On the floor, Batman saw a set of footprints. Robin's footprints! He followed them, first to the barrel where Robin had hidden himself, then towards the centre of the building where they stopped. Dust was kicked up all over the place, as if there had been a struggle.

Then Batman saw something shimmer in the light. It was a large fishhook with a yellow piece of cloth attached to it.

Batman radioed Alfred. "Have you heard from Robin yet?" Batman said into his radio headset.

"I'm afraid not," came Alfred's reply. "One minute he was moping about the Batcave. The next he was gone."

"He went to investigate an alarm in the warehouse district," Batman said. "But there's no sign of him here."

"Another false alarm?" Alfred asked.

"It appears so," Batman said. "But this one was a trap."

"Any clues?" Alfred asked.

"Just one," Batman said.

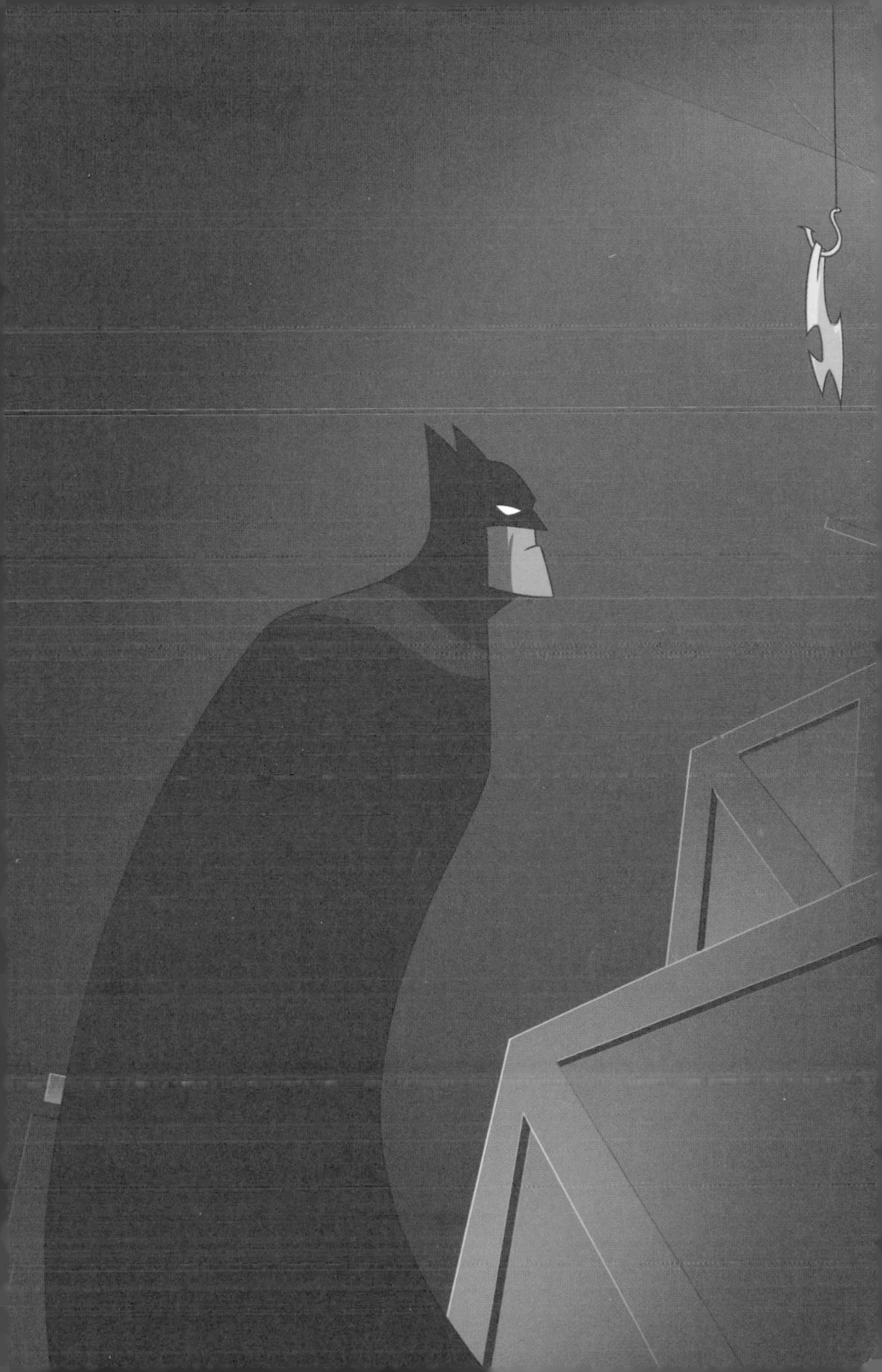

"There's a fishhook with a scrap of Robin's cape on it," Batman said.

"Whoever did this may be after bigger fish, Batman," Alfred warned.

"I know," Batman said. "But we won't discover what happened to Robin unless I take the bait."

"What's next?" Alfred asked.

"I think I'll head down to the docks," Batman said, examining the hook. It was several inches long – the type used for deep-sea fishing.

"Why?" asked Alfred.

"That's where all the big fish are," Batman replied.

CHAPTER 3

THE SURPRISE

"Okay, just a little further, Mr J.," Harley Quinn said. "And no peeking. I don't want you ruining the surprise."

Harley led the blindfolded Joker through a door and into a large, well-lit room.

"This surprise better not be a pie in the face," the Joker warned.

"No, no," Harley assured him. "This is so much better."

Inside, dark curtains were draped across a small stage.

On the other side of the room, seated and facing the stage, were several rows of well-dressed people.

The people watched as Harley Quinn led the Joker on to the stage. But the people didn't run or scream. Ropes bound their legs and hands, and party horns were taped to their mouths. Standing among them were several clowns, holding clubs in their arms.

"Okay, we're almost there," Harley encouraged. "Just a few more steps."

Harley led the Joker to the middle of the stage and had him face the crowd.

"Are you ready for your surprise?" Harley asked.

"Do clowns have rubber noses?" the Joker chuckled.

Harley signalled to a clown standing near the side of the stage. He held up a large sign that read "BLOW!"

SQUEAK! SQUEAK!

The captive people blew on their horns. Honks and buzzes echoed throughout the room. A couple of clowns opened boxes. Suddenly, red and orange and purple and green balloons filled the air.

Harley pulled the blindfold off the Joker's face, and shrieked, "Happy Birthday!"

The Joker looked around at the balloons and the people and laughed. "I didn't even know it was my birthday," he said.

"That's why it's a surprise," said Harley.

The Joker motioned towards the people. "I didn't know I had so many friends, either," he said with an evil grin.

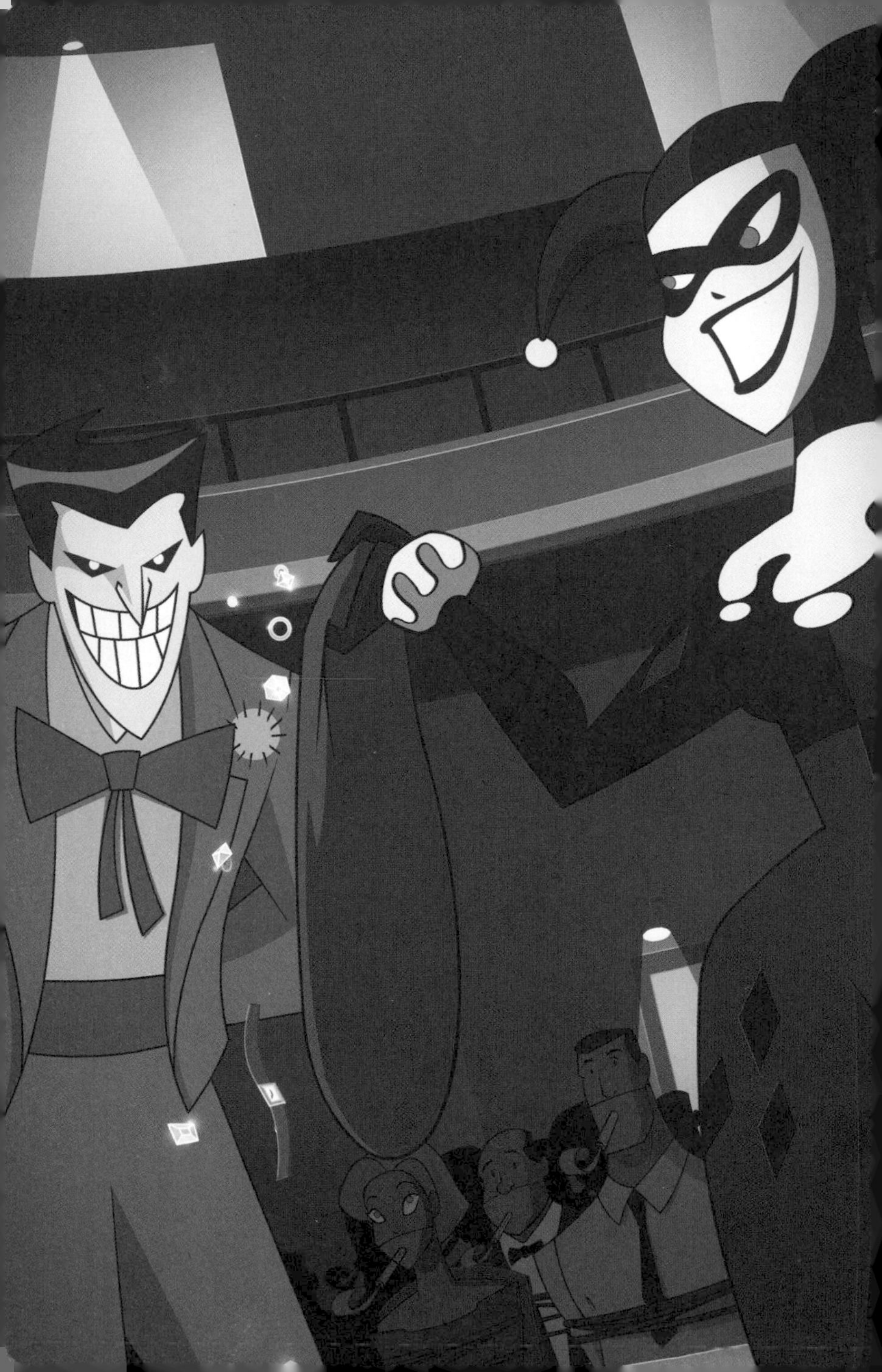

"They even brought gifts," Harley said.

Harley held out a bag full of stolen jewellery and cash to the Joker.

"They seem like a captive audience," the Joker laughed. "Should I tell them a joke?"

"Sure, Mr J. They're *bound* to laugh," Harley said.

"Okay, okay, let me see . . ." the Joker began. "Why can't a clown's nose be twelve inches long?"

The people stared at him blankly.

"Because then it would be a foot!" the Joker snorted.

No one laughed.

Harley scowled at the people for a second. Then she realized that the party horns were still taped to their mouths.

Harley ordered the clowns in the audience to remove them. Then the clown to the side of the stage held up a new sign, which read, "Laugh!" The room filled with frightened, half-hearted laughter.

Harley Quinn looked at the Joker, hoping for his approval.

"Oh, Harley," the Joker gushed. "You're too kind."

"But wait, Mr J.," Harley squealed as she pointed at the curtains. "There's much more!"

The curtains parted, revealing the Boy Wonder. He was dangling above a huge aquarium. Colourful fish, tiger sharks, and electric eels circled above a coral reef.

"Oooh, now that's a shocking surprise!" the Joker squealed with glee.

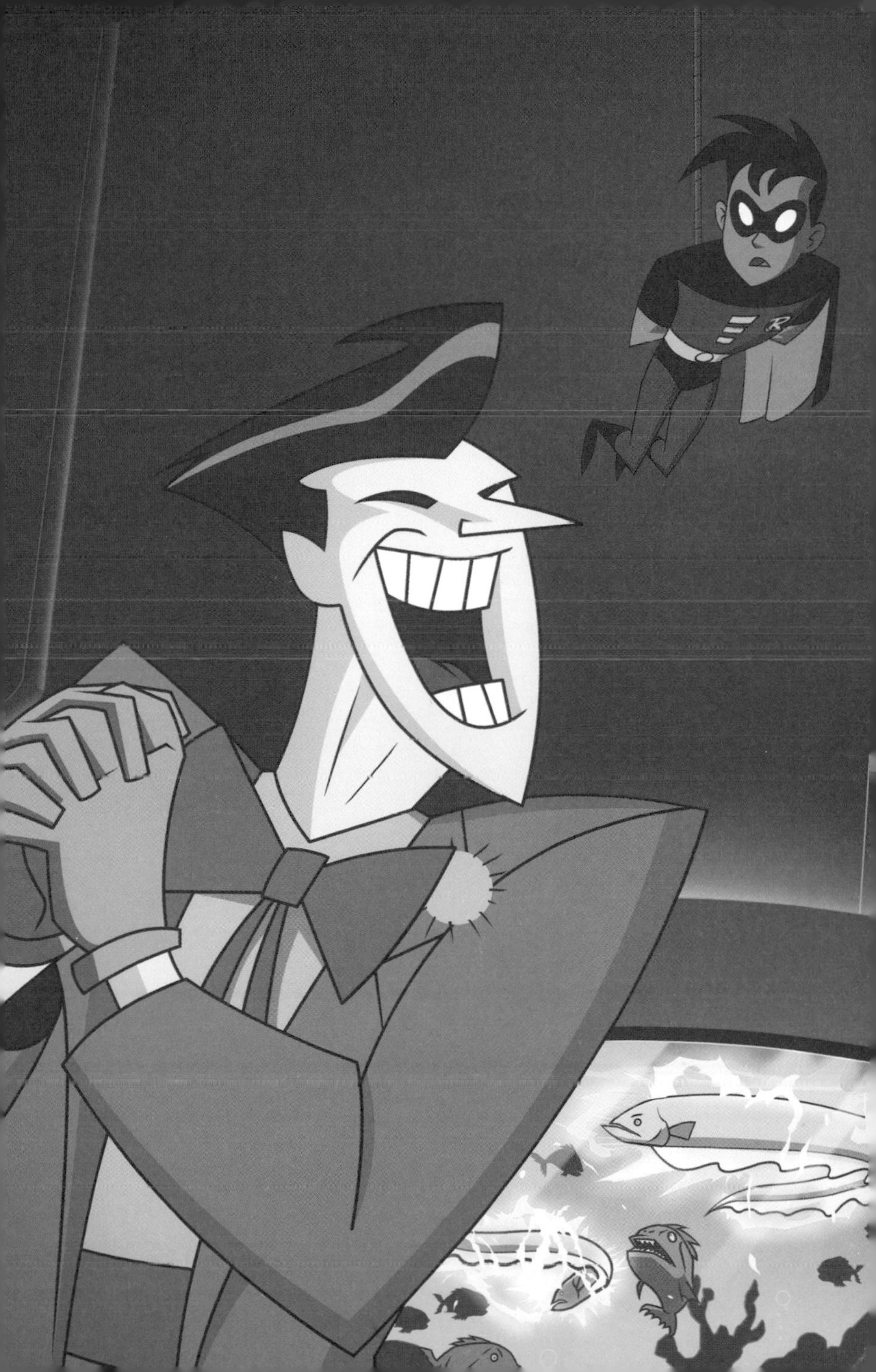

CHAPTER 4

FISHING FOR BATS

At this time of night, the docks were nearly empty. Batman parked the Batcycle behind a shed. He slinked through the shadows, not knowing what he was looking for. He had come here only on a hunch.

Up ahead, near one of the piers, a boat was docking. There was some excited shouting coming from the crew. A couple of men were dragging a third man from the boat. He seemed hurt.

In the distance, Batman could hear the wail of an ambulance siren.

He rushed to see what was wrong.

"Batman!" one of the crew shouted.

Batman looked down at an unconscious man. He was bound tightly in super-strong fishing line.

"What happened to him?" Batman asked.

"We don't know," the crewman replied. "He was tied to the dock."

"We almost hit him with our boat when we came to shore," the other crewman said.

Batman bent down and pulled the gag from the man's mouth. The man moaned in pain. Examining him, Batman noticed that he was breathing okay, even though he was unconscious. The man was also very sunburned, so he had probably been tied up in the sun all day.

Batman cut the man loose with a Batarang and stayed with him until the ambulance arrived. Afterwards, he radioed Alfred.

"Find anything, sir?" Alfred asked.

"I'm not sure, Alfred," Batman replied. "There was a man tied up to one of the docks. But he is unconscious and no one here knows him."

Batman added, "Alfred, could you patch me through to Detective Montoya?"

"Right away, sir," Alfred said.

A second later, Batman heard Renee Montoya's voice on his headset. "We haven't found any clues, yet," she said. "We even tried locating the technician responsible for setting up the alarm system, but he seems to be missing."

"Since when?" Batman asked.

"Since this morning," Renee replied. "His boss says he was called away on some special project, but no one is sure what it was about."

"There was a man tied up at the docks," Batman said. "He could be the missing technician."

As he was talking into his headset, Batman looked down at his feet. He noticed the man's gag lying there, a crumpled piece of paper. Batman picked it up and flattened it out. It was a newspaper article about the new coral reef tank at the aquarium. Tonight was a special showing for the aquarium's wealthy donors. Many of Gotham City's richest and most powerful citizens were going to attend.

"Detective Montoya," Batman said. "Can you send someone to the hospital to talk to this man when he regains consciousness? He may be able to tell us who's behind these events."

"Okay, Batman," Montoya replied.

Tucking the piece of paper away, Batman sprinted to the Batcycle. He revved its engine and sped away into the night.

• • •

At the aquarium, the Joker stood on the stage with a remote in his hand.

"Okay, folks," the Joker said to his captive crowd. "If you aren't going to laugh at my jokes, then I'll have to find other ways to entertain you."

CLICK! He pushed a button, and Robin plunged into the tank.

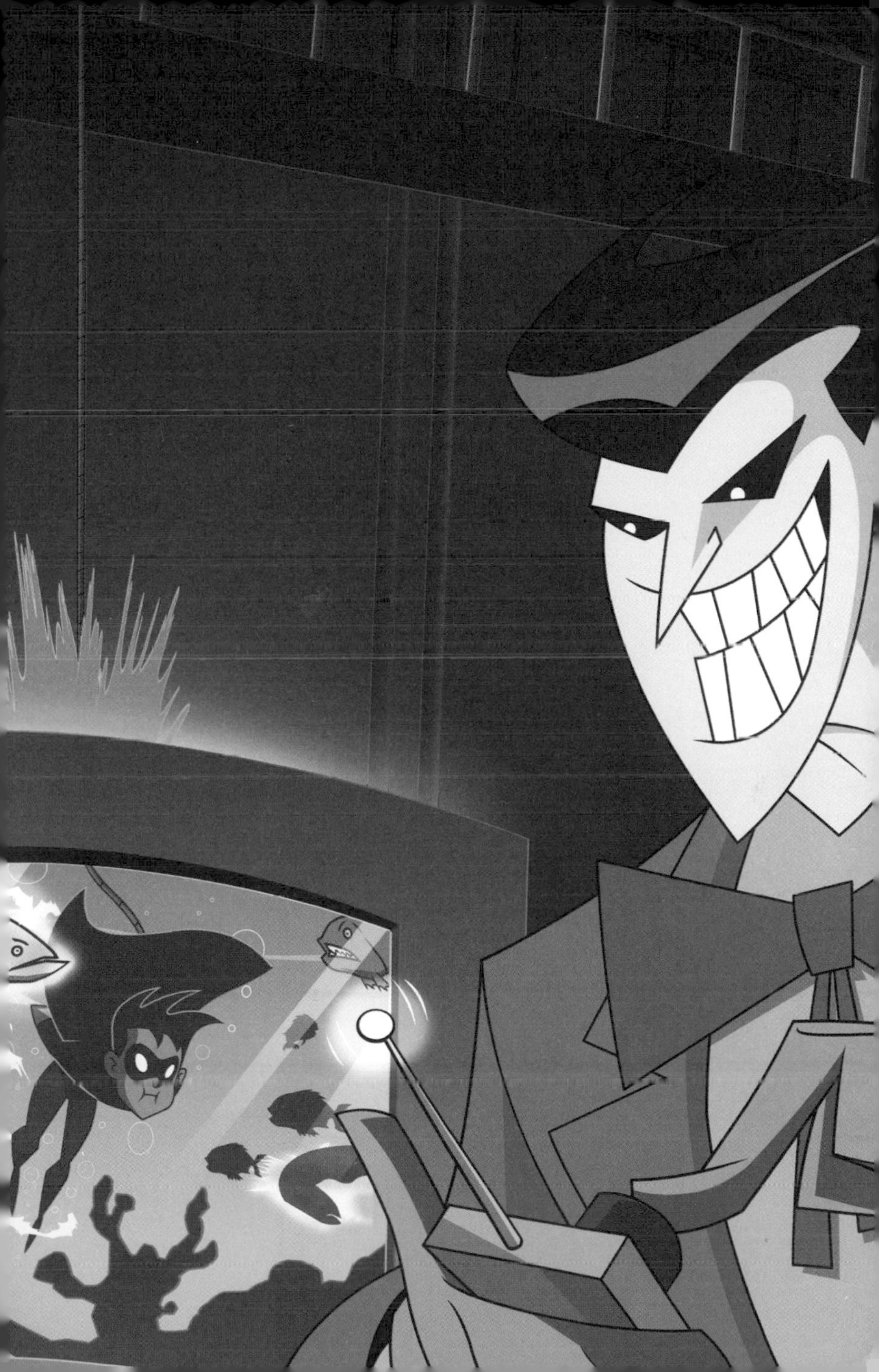

The people in the audience shouted and begged for the Joker to release Robin. But it was obvious that they were tired. Their voices were hoarse from hours of laughing at the Joker's jokes.

"Um, Mr J.," Harley Quinn pointed to the tank. Sharks and electric eels swam near Robin. "The party's not over yet."

"Okay," the Joker pouted.

CLICK! He pushed another button on the remote. Robin was yanked out of the water, gurgling and spluttering.

"Let's try another one," the Joker turned to the crowd. "What's a shark's favourite sandwich?"

The crowd stared, dumbfounded, at the Joker. No one responded.

"Come on, people!" the Joker screamed.

"The Boy Wonder is about to become a shark treat," he threatened.

Still silence from the crowd.

"I know! I know!" Harley raised her hand. "Peanut butter and jellyfish!"

The Joker chuckled. A clown raised the sign to laugh, but the crowd only let loose a half-hearted chuckle.

"Not good enough," the Joker yelled, pushing a button on the remote.

Robin took a deep breath before plunging into the water again. He didn't struggle once he was submerged. He didn't want the sharks to mistake him for prey. If he thrashed around, they might think he was an injured seal or fish.

Robin backed up against the reef. He tried to use the coral to cut the rope.

Robin had to be careful because the coral was razor sharp. If he cut himself, the sharks would smell the blood and attack. He also needed to keep clear of the electric eels. They could deliver a deadly shock if he touched one of them.

"Can I try a joke, Mr J.?" Harley asked.

"Sure," the Joker replied, pushing the button. Robin was yanked out of the water.

Harley turned to the crowd. "What do you get when you cross an electric eel with a sponge?" she asked. After a brief pause, Harley shouted, "A shock absorber!"

No one laughed.

"That's curtains for the Boy Wonder," the Joker said, about to push the button.

"Wait!" Harley Quinn said. "A very special guest will be showing up soon!"

CHAPTER 5

THE ONE THAT GOT AWAY

Batman zipped through the streets on his Batcycle. He knew something was fishy about the chain of events that had led him back and forth across town. He would never have guessed that they would lead him to the Gotham City Aquarium.

It all added up: The heist at the Pearl Emporium, the van from Fish 'N' Stuff that had made him late in meeting Robin, the hook at the warehouse where Robin had disappeared – they were all connected somehow.

Then there was the man tied up at the docks, and lastly, the flyer that was used to gag him. It was like one big practical joke was being played on him.

When Batman neared the aquarium, he circled around to the back. He parked the Batcycle behind a shed and sneaked around the aquarium to a side entrance.

Quietly, Batman slipped through the door. It was dark inside, but he could hear laughter echoing down the hallway. It was a familiar laugh – one that made him fear for Robin's life.

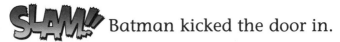 Batman kicked the door in.

"Look, Harley!" the Joker shrieked. "It's a party crasher."

"Not quite, Mr J.," Harley squealed. "It's the catch of the day."

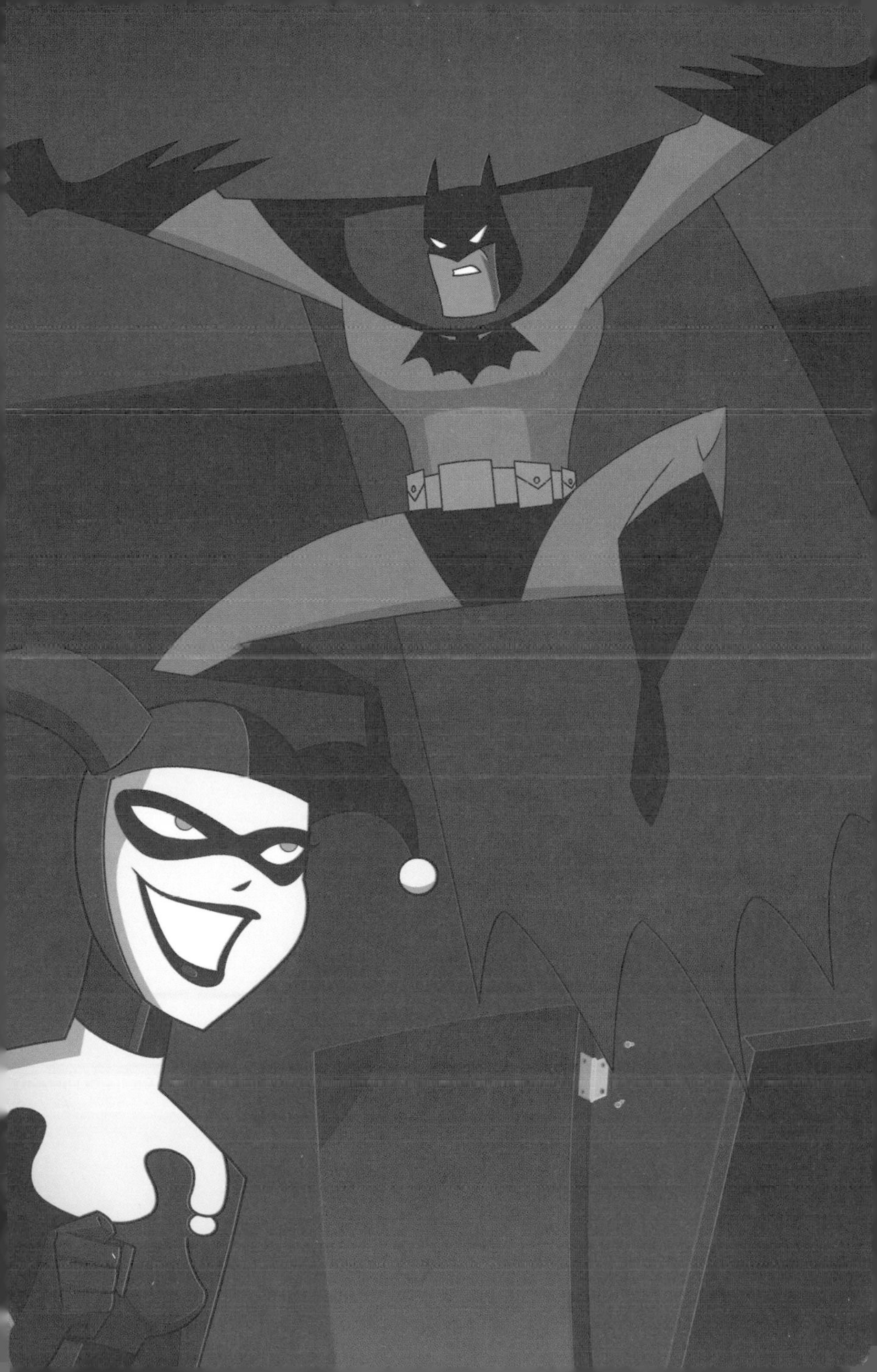

Harley looked over to one of the clowns who stood near the doorway. On the wall next to him was a rope, which was connected to a very large metal ball.

"You fell right into my trap, Batman," Harley laughed. "Hook, line . . . "

Harley pushed a button on the remote. A spotlight blinded Batman. Then the clown by the door cut the rope.

". . . and sinker!" she screamed.

The metal ball began to drop.

Even though Batman was blinded by the spotlight, he heard a gasp from the crowd. Robin yelled, "It's a trap!"

Instinctively, Batman jumped aside. **CRASH!!** The ball smashed into the wall just inches away from him.

Its impact shook the floor, knocking Batman to the ground. Instantly, several of the clowns jumped on Batman, swinging wildly with their clubs.

The distraction of the ball allowed Robin to slip his hands free of the ropes. With a quick kick of his legs, he started to swing back and forth. By the time the clowns attacked Batman, Robin had gained enough momentum to swing beyond the tank. He let go of the rope and flew towards the combatants, knocking over a couple of the clowns as he landed. He quickly helped Batman to his feet.

The Dynamic Duo stood back-to-back, surrounded by several clowns.

"And I thought *you* needed rescuing," Batman said.

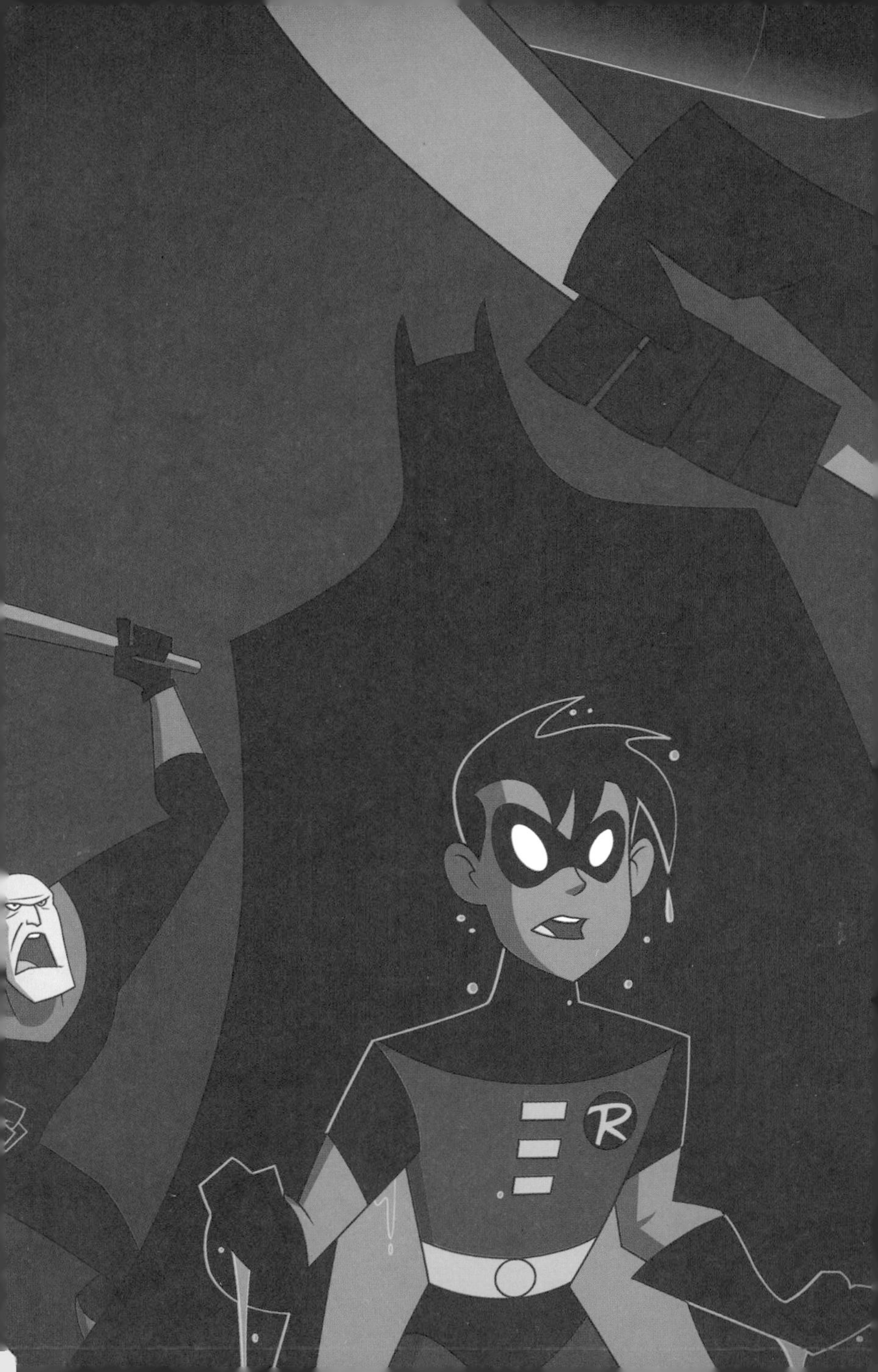

"I had it all under control," Robin said, smiling. "I was just waiting for you to even the odds a little."

Just then, one of the clowns swung his club at Robin. The Boy Wonder ducked and kicked out a foot, tripping the clown and knocking him to the ground. **THUD!**

Two clowns charged Batman. Batman blocked one's punch and grabbed a club from him. Twirling around, Batman used the club to hit the other clown in the stomach, doubling him over. Then he smashed his elbow into the first clown, knocking him to the ground. **KA-POW!**

Several more clowns attacked, clubs swinging. Batman whirled and punched. Robin dodged and kicked. Soon, two more clowns had been knocked to the ground.

Behind the combatants, Harley Quinn grabbed the Joker's arm. She pulled him towards a door on the other side of the room.

"Come on, Mr J.," she whimpered. "This party's over."

"It was a blast," the Joker teased. "But next year, just get me a singing telegram."

"Anything you say, Mr J.," Harley replied.

The pair ran through the door and disappeared.

Shortly afterwards, Batman and Robin finished the fight. All of the clowns that hadn't run off with the Joker and Harley Quinn had been captured.

Robin untied the audience while Batman called Detective Montoya.

When Montoya arrived, she had paramedics tend to the former captives.

As the Dynamic Duo left the aquarium, Robin turned towards Batman. "Do you know what type of sharks you shouldn't gamble with?" Robin asked.

"No," Batman said.

"Card sharks!" Robin laughed. "Get it? Gamble . . . cards . . . "

As they walked outside, Batman frowned at his partner. "And where did you hear that one?"

"From the Joker," Robin replied. "He had a million of them. Want to hear another?"

"Do I have a choice?" Batman asked.

"What's a shark's favourite kind of school?" Robin asked.

After a brief pause, the Boy Wonder answered, "A school of fish!"

VROOOOOM! VROOOOOM!

Batman got on the Batcycle and revved the engine to drown out the bad jokes.

When Robin had stopped speaking, Batman said, "I'll give you a ride back to your scooter if you promise not to tell any jokes on the way."

"Okay," Robin said as he hopped on behind Batman. "But I need to practice them for my presentation about coral reefs on Friday. These jokes will have my classmates glued to their seats."

"In other words, you hope to have a captive audience," Batman chuckled.

Together, the Dynamic Duo zoomed away into the dawn of a new day.

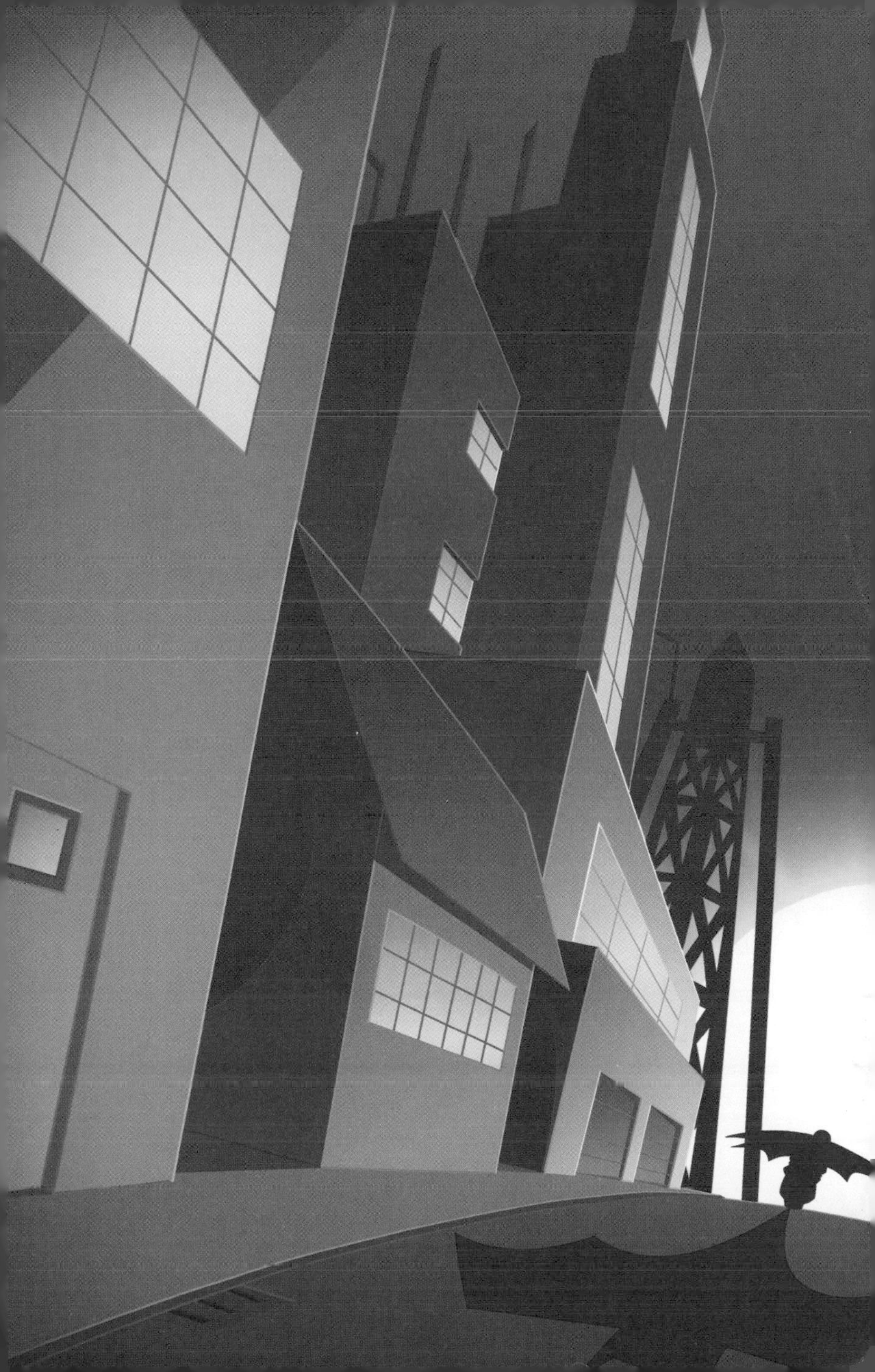

Quinn, Harley

REAL NAME: Dr Harleen Quinzel

OCCUPATION: Professional criminal

BASE: Gotham City

HEIGHT:
5 feet, 7 inches

WEIGHT:
10 stone

EYES:
Blue

HAIR:
Blonde

Dr Harleen Quinzel was once a successful psychiatrist working at Arkham Asylum. When she met the Joker, everything changed. His heartbreaking, but false, stories about his childhood won Harley's heart. Soon after, Quinzel was caught helping the Joker escape Arkham Asylum, and she was given a padded cell of her own. Now she clowns around Gotham as Harley Quinn, the Joker's partner in crime.

G.C.P.D. GOTHAM CITY POLICE DEPARTMENT

- An Olympic-level gymnast, Harley possesses exceptional agility and quickness. Her high-flying acrobatics and quick feet make her a slippery crook to catch.

- Harley is completely obsessed with her boyfriend, the Joker. They have a troubled relationship, but they always end up back together after a fight.

- Harley and the Joker have two vicious pet hyenas named Bud and Lou, whom Harley affectionately calls their "babies." They were handpicked by the Clown Queen because of the constant chuckling sounds they make.

- Super-villainesses Harley Quinn and Poison Ivy befriended each other after one of Harley's many quarrels with the Joker. As a gift, Poison Ivy injected Harley with a serum that gave her immunity to all poisons! They joined forces as the Queens of Crime, and they were successful in many high-profile heists.

CONFIDENTIAL

BIOGRAPHIES

Blake A. Hoena began by writing stories about trolls lumbering around in the woods behind his parents' house. Later, he gained a Masters of Fine Arts degree in Creative Writing. Since graduating, Blake has written more than thirty books for children. Most recently, he has been working on a series of graphic novels about two space alien brothers, Eek and Ack, who are determined to conquer Earth.

Dan Schoening has had a passion for animation and comic books from an early age. Currently, Dan does freelance work in the animation and game industry and spends a lot of time with his lovely little daughter, Paige.

GLOSSARY

captive kept in confinement or restraints, or paying close attention

combatant person involved in a struggle or a fight

compartments separate parts of a container used for storing specific things

dynamic energetic and good at getting things done

habitat place and natural conditions where a plant or animal lives

half-hearted without much enthusiasm or interest

momentum force or speed of an object while moving

suspicious feel that something is wrong

unconscious not awake or able to see, feel, or think

Utility Belt Batman's belt, which holds all of his weaponry and gadgets

waning becoming smaller or weaker

DISCUSSION QUESTIONS

1. Robin does his homework in the Batcave. Where do you do your homework? What is your favourite class?

2. After Robin is kidnapped, Batman discovers several clues to his whereabouts. What were some of the fishy hints that led to his location at the aquarium?

3. Who was the bigger hero in this story – Batman or Robin? Why?

WRITING PROMPTS

1. Harley kidnaps Robin and gives him to the Joker as a birthday present. What's the best gift you've ever received? Why did you like it?

2. Batman and Robin team up to fight crime. Who would you choose to be your super hero partner? Why would he or she make a good teammate? Write about it.

3. Harley and the Joker are both evil clown super-villains. Think up your own clown and name him or her. What does it look like? What superpowers does it have? Draw a picture of your clown.